SOUL
SWEET

SOUL SWEET

A SOULFUL COLLECTION OF POETRY FROM THE HEART

GWENDOLYN HARRELL- OYEWOLE

PALMETTO
PUBLISHING
Charleston, SC
www.PalmettoPublishing.com

Copyright © 2024 by Gwendolyn Harrell- Oyewole

All rights reserved.

No portion of this book may be reproduced, stored in a retrieval system, or transmitted in any form by any means—electronic, mechanical, photocopy, recording, or other—except for brief quotations in printed reviews, without prior permission of the author.

Paperback ISBN: 9798822966604

I dedicate these poems and words of wisdom to all the strong, brilliant women of our family, but a special thanks to three industrious women: Katie Harrell Tremble, (my mother), Annie Laura Harrell (my mother's mom who has now moved to heaven), and Susie R. Harrell, (my favorite cousin). These women showed me how to live and gave me a purpose for living. I am eternally grateful for their undying love, support and encouragement.

I thank God for allowing me to be born into the best family on planet earth. Much love to my siblings, Melvin and Marvin (twins), Barbara, McKinney, Brenda (my birthday mate 11-16), and Carl; children (Danielle and Damaian); grandchildren, great-grandchildren, family members, my true friends, colleagues (former and present). This life would be so different without your influences.

TABLE OF CONTENTS

LOVE AND LOSS IX
- A BLAZING FONDUE AFFAIR 1
- A LATE NIGHT RAIN 2
- A LOVER AND A FRIEND 3
- ACROSS THE WATER 4
- "B" 5
- CHOCOLATE 6
- EIGHT O' CLOCK 7
- ENTWINED 8
- GLIMPSE OF TRUTH 9
- I LONG 10
- I MS U! 11
- KON-TIKKI'S SPELLBINDING ESCAPE 12
- LEFTOVER LOVE 14
- MAIL MAN 15
- MAIL ME 16
- MIDNIGHT HEIR 17
- ONENESS 18
- THERE IS SOMEONE FOR EVERYONE 19
- WITHOUT YOU 21

MIRACLES AND FEARS 23
- DIVORCE 25

EMOTIONAL KAMIKAZE · 26
FOR FEAR · 27
GHETTO GUY · 28
HURT · 29
I COULDN'T SLEEP · 30
THE GLOOMY BLAHS · 31
USER · 32
WILL YOU STILL LOVE ME? · · · · · · · · · · · · · · · · 33
WONDER WHY · 34
WORTH VISUALIZED AND YOUR LOSS · · · · 35

ADMIRATIONS · 37
A GOLDEN HEART · 39
ALONG MY WAY · 40
A NOISE IN THE PARK · 42
CRIMSON HANDS · 43
DANI ELLE DANIELLE DANIELLE · · · · · · · · · · · 45
DEE LAMONT · 46
GUIDE MY THOUGHTS WELL · · · · · · · · · · · · · · 47
MASTERPIECE OF INNER PEACE · · · · · · · · · · · 48
MIRACLE GIFT · 49
MY BEST FRIEND · 50
ODE TO MY FAVORITE PEN · · · · · · · · · · · · · · · · 51
ORANGE SUNSHINE BRIGHT · · · · · · · · · · · · · · 52
SATURDAY, WHAT A DAY · · · · · · · · · · · · · · · · · · 53

LOVE AND LOSS

A BLAZING FONDUE AFFAIR

He makes me dizzy.
I can't wait to see him.
My insides flutter into a melt,
Whenever I hear his voice.

Mix me up, scramble my thoughts, and
Cook me through and through.
Boiled, over easy, and sometimes two.
Pure, soft, whipped and creamy.
Oh, how do you like your fondue?

Mixed together and brought to a boil,
A scrumptious mixture wrapped in foil.

A LATE NIGHT RAIN

Rain
Rain
Rain
Pounding on my window pane.
Wind
Wind
Wind
Howling over and over and again
A kiss
A kiss
A kiss
Oh, so softly a gentle kiss.
Yes
Yes
Yes
Oh, what a beautiful rainy late night kiss
Pounding and howling on my window pane.

A LOVER AND A FRIEND

What we have is "Magic" from above
All because we are both in love,
I pray this is real, not just a joke
That won't be fulfilled.
I love you and you love me,
Together we are thee
You and me.

ACROSS THE WATER

Never have I encountered a human species of this sort.
You are truly a unique Homo sapien.
Henceforth and now, I love your characteristics,
Personality, intellect, physique, mental stability and candid views.

You are an asset to my life.
You are sunshine to a stormy day.
You possess a character never developed in most.
You are sweet, kind and gentle.
I can't believe there's another anywhere like you.
 In your eyes are the reflections of tomorrow.

The beard covering your face has speckles of wisdom.
How could I have not seen you for who you really are?
You are my PROMISED one.

"B"

You walked in,
You walked out.
We both knew it would come to this.
I guess you've written me off your list,
And sent me on without even a kiss.

I walked in,
I walked out.
We both knew this was not my wish,
But boy oh boy, you will be missed.

I walked in, you walked in.
I walked out, you walked out.

OH what a minor BLISS,
To once have loved and now be missed.

CHOCOLATE

When you needed somethin' sweet
In this awesome heat.
Remember Dunkin Donuts with a Chocolate glaze for
only
"Two "O" Six.

You
Me
And
Chocolate!
Oh, what a fix.
Who else knows the chocolate trick.

EIGHT O' CLOCK

On our first night together,
You evoked a stir.
And I must agree,
You were a "PERFECT" sir.

ENTWINED

Your present is always
Entwined with your past.
You love what you have,
But miss what you had.

You know what you're in,
But wonder what it would be like
To be in something else.
You see now, but you can't block out
What you've seen.

You feel now, but you can't forget what you've felt.
You hear now, but you can't erase what you've heard.
You weep now, but you can't really know why you wept.

You know what you are,
But you wonder what you've been.
You take what you have, and miss what you don't.

GLIMPSE OF TRUTH

Let it go, let him go.
Stop the pain.
It isn't worth it.
He isn't worth it.
The pain certainly
Isn't worth it.

You can't be with him.
He can't be with you.
Let it go and the problem will go.

It's hard letting go.
It's even harder staying.
Staying where? Wherever?

It's hard letting go.
But once in a while,
You get a faint glimpse of the truth.
So, simply let it go!

I LONG

I long for someone to say
How much they sincerely care
To give me that special glance and
Caress me in a delicate way.
To bring me flowers, even if it isn't a special day.
Someone to say "Hi' beautiful;
Someone who will know when things are in disarray.
I long for someone to make my day.
I long and long and long…I hope these longs will come my way.

I MS U!

Why haven't you called?
You promised you would.
Somehow I knew your promise was without merit.

Once, in a time, long ago,
I wrote, "Time Flows" yet
My love for you goes and goes.
After carefully scrutinizing this
Aged picture of you, it brings
To my mind my sincerest feelings for you.

Although I know you are only a telephone call away,
And hours of miles away. I can't convince myself to actively
Seek communications.
Sometimes I feel so empty and shallow inside,
I feel as though you have gone and left me for eternity.
Will you ever know just how much I MS U?

KON-TIKKI'S SPELLBINDING ESCAPE
St. Thomas Virgin Island, 2002

Once upon the island's waterfront,
Juliette and I happened upon a tall, striking personage in search of five tickets:
Needed for five friends and self,
For a late night ocean tramp;
To board the open-aired, glass-bottomed party boat.
Destined for fun, fun, fun,
On the Atlantic O-c-e-a-n;
Only a three-hour run.
Hailing the sea without the excruciating sun, sun, sun,
Only a three-hour run.

A swooshing, swishing, rock around the peninsula;
Passing purely through passion for a rendezvous
with an angelic god or goddess' destiny.
Only a three-hour run.

Whisking through the wind, wandering, waving, and waging
a roar of tumultuous embers of oceanic stirrrrrrrrrr.
Only a three-hour run.

Enthralling and enchanting an adventure,
Leaving him and her speechless, spellbound and splendidly in love.
A late night, St Thomas Escape,
evoking and charging a rousing purrrrrrrr.
Merely a three-hour run.
In search of … a three hour run!

LEFTOVER LOVE

When you can't have her then you remember me.
When she doesn't want you then you remember me.
When she doesn't make you happy anymore,
then you remember I might.
You spend all important occasions with her,
and I am not remembered as someone you might give a glance
or even a second chance.
You work two and three jobs just to maintain,
So that you can ease your pain.
Left out in the cold trying not to be a leftover love.

MAIL MAN

The male with the mail.
I wait anxiously to see what you will bring.
Juan Curtis what a name?
They seem as if they are one in the same.
I just seem to be one wacky dame,
Who digs such a peculiar name.

MAIL ME

12. 5   Size Shoe
A Kiss on the Cheek

Two friendly Hugs
Many Handshakes

Numerous brushes up against and a personal check.

MIDNIGHT HEIR

The water is so peaceful and calm tonight. I can hear constant chitter chatter of people's voices. I hear boat engines whining down, there is a certain stillness in the midnight air. Although I see many faces, none of these resemble one strand of hair on your head. I have to force myself to reject the images constantly interrupting my thoughts as I write these lines.

The sky is black and dark and looks as though the blue will never shine through. Far away in the distance, I hear the turbine rumbling of an aircraft's engine, and think what fun it must be to soar the heavens on a bleak desolate night.

The wind weaving back and forth across my face and through my hair sends a certain chill down my spine. Not a death chill, but a relief from the heat chill. Couples sitting together holding hands conversing is a most picturesque scene.

I wonder why everyone else seems to have so much happiness love and joy. What would I give for one moment of true and unrelenting love? I mean true love that is able to withstand all the violent blows of life, and all the pleasant aromas of fresh air in the late midnight air.

ONENESS

One heart
One soul
One mind
One thought
Divine.

Two hearts
Two souls
Two minds
Two thoughts
Divine.

One sign
One love
DIVINE.

THERE IS SOMEONE FOR EVERYONE

Many men and women look around at another person's happiness and wonder why not me?
That's exactly right, why not you?

But, you should also ask yourself another question.
Why should it be you?
Remember, there are two sides to every coin!

After careful consideration, I have come to the conclusion that there is someone for everyone. You simply may not have met that person, but that does not change the fact that there is someone for you. He or she could be in another situation, another city, another state, or in another universe, but that is another subject. Just know that the GOD we serve is too great to create you without the perfect mate.

Of course, those of you who have not met that perfect mate yet, want to know; who, what, when and where?
Who really knows?
There is an answer to that question, but the answer lies within.

You may meet HIM or HER in this lifetime, but on the other hand, you may not.
Who really knows?

WITHOUT YOU

What is a bagel without cream cheese, or a stanza without a line?
What is a chirp without a bird, or a sentence without a word?
What is a present without a past, or an entrance without an exit?
What is a flower without a bud, or a night without a day?
What is a husband without a wife, or a child without love?
What is the south without the north, or the mind without the thought?
What is knowledge without wisdom, or hate without love?
What is a body without a heart, or a foe without a friend?
What is a king without a queen, or a mountain without a peak?
What is a sunrise without a sunset, or an earth without a universe?
What is a team without a dream?
What are we without HE (HIM)?

MIRACLES AND FEARS

DIVORCE

Divorce is an ugly thing. It separates a man and a woman, but worst of all it separates children from their parents. God intended for children to have both parents, but what happens in a divorce?
Daughters are forced to leave their fathers and live in the shadows of only their mothers; never learning the ultimate bonds of father and daughter.
Sons are forced to leave their father, living only in the silhouette of their mother; forever hungering for that dominant male role model.
Divorce is an ugly thing; rearing its head like and unrelenting serpent that slithers and strikes at the most inopportune time.

EMOTIONAL KAMIKAZE

On today…Off tomorrow
Yes…No
Maybe…Maybe Not
Up…No…Down
Left…Right
Forward…Reverse
Come…Leave…Now…Later
Front…Rear
Enter…Exit
Good…Bad
Light…Dark
Black…White
Right…Wrong
Old…New
Start…Finish
Stop and let go of this Emotional Kamikaze

FOR FEAR

Fear of the unknown is very scary
What we don't know shouldn't hurt us but it does.
I fear change. I fear life and I fear death.
Change is unknown
Life is unknown and death is unknown.
There's no wonder we fear all these unknowns.

GHETTO GUY

You can take the boy out of the ghetto,
But you can't take the ghetto out of the boy!
I married this guy!
Oh somebody, Please, Please, Please!
Tell me why,
I would marry such a ghetto guy?

HURT

It's just a little trial
You encounter for a while.
Mild, pointed and sharp
Sometimes as heavy as a harp.

This little trial, will only last for a small while.
WHAT IS THIS? ONLY A LITTLE HURT.

I COULDN'T SLEEP

Pondering thoughts unable to sleep.
I pray the Lord my soul to keep.
Keep me strong
Keep me safe
Keep me healthy and keep me here
And please allow me never to weep.

THE GLOOMY BLAHS

Gloomy, dark and unsuspecting
You creep into our lives.
Worse than a thief in the night,
You steal away any hope for joy.

Havoc and turmoil are your constant
Companions and partners in crime.
Crying, trembling, and fear are ominous cousins that
constantly lend you an ear.
Escape back into the dark, gloomy abyss from whence
you came.

USER

We all play the fool,
Sometimes like a tool.
When we don't accept a rule,
We're tossed out like a spool.

When you needed me nothing could prevent thee,
From being in my company
Practically, Daily and Constantly.

Now that you have what you need,
It's time to take your leave,
And continue on to the next victim and deed.

WILL YOU STILL LOVE ME?

I was thinking just the other day.
Will you still love me when I'm old and gray?
Will you still love me when my skin is no longer free
from wrinkles?
Will you still love me when I can't seem to get around
the same old way?
Will you still love me when it becomes another day?
Will you still love me when I can't iron, wash and cook,
Or will I just sit and wither away,
Promising to write that one special book?
Will you still love me?
When my thoughts run away?
Or will it become someone else, some other on
another given day?

WONDER WHY

Have you ever wondered how the
skyscrapers of the past, were built, buildings such as the
pyramids?
These buildings were not only built millions of years ago,
but ironically they are still standing.

Have you ever wondered what the eye on the pyramid on
the back of the dollar means?
Have you ever wondered if there is another creature;
as knowledgeable as humans?
Have you ever wondered what makes me different from
you?
Is it because we are from different birth canals?
Have you ever wondered why you speak with an accent
and I don't?
Have you ever wondered why my hair is kinky and yours
is straight?
Have you ever wondered the color of GOD?
Well, if you have wondered all these things, then you are
as human as I.
My God will not give me the answer until he is positive
that I will be able to accept the answers.
Seek God for all the answers.
Eventually you will find the most obvious one.

WORTH VISUALIZED AND YOUR LOSS

I am a capable worthwhile strong intelligent vibrant person.
I am fulfilled successful and prosperous in everything I do.
If you decide not to visualize my worth and potential.
If you decide to converse with another when clearly you wanted to speak with me.
It is your loss.

When you needed my strength and decided at the last moment you could go the distance.
Because it gave you room to boast; you frowned upon a helping hand.
You say your consummate pride overshadows your will and chauvinism shoving you about and not realizing whether you are in or out.
Listen; do not listen.
If you want to call and don't,
If you want to buy flowers
If you want to hold me gently
If you want to tell me I am special
If you want to give me a passionate kiss

If you want my confidence and companionship through a friendship.
For whatever it is that made you think you could go the distance without my persistence; truly it is your LOSS.

ADMIRATIONS

A GOLDEN HEART

Warm, friendly, and elegant
Is the person of whom I speak?
A friend in all her endeavors,
She'll never let you down,
Regardless of what life you seek.

Small but fragile is her peaceful character
I pray will one day rub off on me.
Once you have encountered such a delicate individual,
You'll be apt to pursue a friend with such a beautiful gift,
A treasure needed to give you a certain lift

Once you encounter such an individual,
You will have a glimpse of a lady with a golden heart.

ALONG MY WAY
(For a Native Fraternity Brother)

Elation
Vibration
Emancipation-Proclamation,
 Manifestation
What a joyous Revelation.

You have come to pass and freed my brothers and sisters at last. No longer do we wear the mask: my people's oppression is a thing of the past.

On behalf of honest Ole Abe,
You twisted and turned and even paved
The perilous journey along the way.
Some may say: nay, nay, nay!
But, it is because of you James Weldon Johnson
That my destiny is on its way.

Six years after such a momentous event,
That's when my Creator thought you should be sent.
Intentionally if not meant,
To become a beacon of light and hope
For all those who must learn to cope.
The immortal words in your song,

"Lift Ev'ry Voice and Sing," ring out true many wondrous things
From our African ancestors and tribal kings.
Hope, triumph and joy
Hope, triumph and joy
Reverberate through my inner core.
The faith from my past has taught me,
To open my eyes and see, the wondrous fruits of majesty!

With a mission in mind only to write a song,
To commemorate the Late Abe Lincoln. You,
Along with your brother and later friend,
Augusta Savage; single-handedly united our race
And cemented our bond. Thanks, my native –Jacksonville (FL) brother for all that you have done. "We will forever hold you dear" and promote your grand legacy.

A NOISE IN THE PARK

Where are you?
In the trees
On the branches
Or are you underneath,
The mulch surrounding the base of the tree?
Creak, creak, creak, and chirp, chirp, chirp…
Just where are you anyway?

CRIMSON HANDS

At a bustling breakfast diner one April morning, I stole a glance at a pair of Crimson Hands.

Unbeknownst to the owner of these agile crimson hands, my thoughts and imagination ran wild as I watched this elderly sojourner make a telephone call using his elongated fingers. As he pressed each number, my mind actively leapt from the first number to the last number. Hawkish, I then listened extremely close as these hands revealed a poignant tale. They shared their legacy of life and before my very own eyes; they un-blanketed their past experiences.

They spoke of their excruciating labor through coal mines, arduous hours in the cotton fields tobacco patches and even the orange orchards. They sang the song of split wood, roped cattle, bailed hay and mixed mortar. These hands appeared to have engaged in bloody battles and wars. No task or job was beyond their reach. Nothing seemed too great or too small. Upon closer observation, every wrinkle relinquished another awesome mystery. One even greater than the one just before.

These were the hands that built bridges, sky scrapers, and

other historical monuments. There was nothing these hands could not do. Although they appear to be old and tired, there is much to do before they actually retire. Whatever it is, it will be just another journey, just another story, on just another day.

DANI ELLE
DANIELLE
DANIELLE

My parallel
Clad in royal blue
You are also one of the two
I knew you would come through.
As I lay lifeless and full of unrest; Your generosity and
kindness permeated the ultimate test. A sacrifice so
unselfish. You turned your mother's wildest dream into a
beautiful wish; Danielle, continue your awesome parallel.

DEE LAMONT

What can I say, but I love you?
And want the best for you,
You are one of the two!

Tried,
Tied,
True,

And sometimes Blue.
Boy, do I certainly do love you!

GUIDE MY THOUGHTS WELL

As the heavy rains bellow profusely from the flickering celestial abodes, all my thoughts of you illuminate as a shriek of light flashes through the ubiquitous sky.

Will you enter my door tonight and caress me gently in your strong, masculine, firm, sinewy arms?

Will you place upon my aching and awaiting lips, a warm passionate and sensuous kiss?

Will you snatch a piece of my desperately wounded heart, or will you simply through your embrace, mold and fashion me into a workable piece of clay?

Will you seduce me tenderly with your erogenous stare?
And make me gasp for a cool breath of fresh air.
Or will you simply love me and leave me without even a care?

MASTERPIECE OF INNER PEACE

Where two clouds meet,
High above the ocean and the sea.
My mind pulls me and lures me into a world,
Altogether different from the world just above.

There is stillness and a peaceful calm clamoring in my head.
I'm in touch with a being much greater than myself.
And I will enjoy all that is left between me and the clouds above.
Float away inner peace and dissolve into a fine masterpiece.

MIRACLE GIFT

Water so pure how have you managed to endure.
Year after year you never cease to be here.
You help me clear my thoughts and look back
on all the things that I have taught.
Flow through the rivers of my soul and help me to unfold
your vigor, lust and lore
For you are the one to make an ominous roar from
the great Jehovah God above.
HE is the answer to our ultimate love.
His son Jesus brought it from above,
By the way of a mighty white dove.
Jesus is my one true love.

MY BEST FRIEND

Hard or soft,
In black, blue, green and red.
You are simply beautiful.
No matter what I say to you,
Or where I end up leaving you,
Whenever I pick you up,
You are always still the same.

Sometimes I get upset because you are bound,
But, I promise never to let you down or toss you on the ground.
We ride together (in silence of course),
Fall asleep together and sit in the park.
You never deserted me or left me alone.
And as long as I have the ability to see,
You will forever be an intricate part of me.

ODE TO MY FAVORITE PEN

To my constant flow of ink,
You have served me well.
You gave me a permanent link.
I'm sorry you're now on the blink.
You served me well, I do tell.
Oh well,
I do tell! My favorite pen.

ORANGE SUNSHINE BRIGHT

I love sunshine.
I love the bright, bright, hot, hot sun.
Piercing through my skin and bathing my face and arms.
Far off in the distance, distance.
You beam in and out of my existence.
No resistance, no resistance.
Bright, bright, bright!
Light, light, light!
Nothing feels this right, bright light.
You are my sun! Sun, sun, sun!

SATURDAY, WHAT A DAY

I've waited on you all week.
Now that you have finally arrived,
I just can't seem to enjoy you at all.
I sleep late and even chance to procrastinate.
I wander far and near, and toss and turn.
Before you know it all has ended with a ball.
My, my, my SATURDAY; you've come and gone.

www.ingramcontent.com/pod-product-compliance
Lightning Source LLC
LaVergne TN
LVHW012036060526
838201LV00061B/4639